LIFE IN THE
FAST LANE

L. SUSAN CABRERA

First Printing February 2005

Printed in the United States of America.

Books by L. Susan Cabrera:
    The Morning Star, Inspirational Poems
    Life in the Fast Lane, Contemporary Poems

L. Susan Cabrera
Post Office Box 334
Capitola, CA 95010

www.LSCabrera.com

ISBN 0-9766489-1-1

To my dear brother
Richard M. Cabrera
who has been my constant friend
and guardian angel.

Contents

Preface

I was born, raised, and lived much of my life in the beautiful city of Palo Alto, California. Palo Alto sits on the fringe of "the world's first high technology region." Three blocks from where I grew up, two young men, Bill Hewlett and Dave Packard, began developing the audio oscillator in their small residential garage back in 1938. The state refers to this historic site as "the birthplace of Silicon Valley."

Silicon Valley has been the start-up location of many innovative, renowned and lucrative high technology companies such as Hewlett-Packard, Intel, Advanced Micro Devices, Google, Varian, Yahoo, Apple, Cisco Systems, and eBay. Along with the stimulation and excitement of such ventures can come round-the-clock hours, fierce competition, financial pressures, and no time or energy for family, friends and self.

Whether we live in Silicon Valley or elsewhere in our country, our many obligations as employees, family members, friends and citizens can be overwhelming. Before we know it, our lives are passing us by and we haven't really had the chance to live them. It's so easy to be thrown off balance and lose sight of who we are as human beings.

I enjoyed writing these poems which take a mindful and humorous look at some of the dilemmas we create by our fast-paced lives. I hope you enjoy <u>Life in the Fast Lane</u>.

Susan Cabrera
January 2005

Special thanks to
my friend Patsy (Fenerin) Luniewski
who reviews my manuscripts
and
my friend James A. Thalmann
who provides technical assistance.

Susan

My Body Won't Cooperate!

I take it here. I take it there.
Exhaustion's near. Can't find a chair.
Don't get much sleep. I eat too late.
My body won't cooperate!

I take it up. I take it down.
The coffee cup's always around.
Caffeine's the way I stay awake.
My body won't cooperate!

I take it right. I take it left.
No time for meals. I am bereft.
When I see food, I salivate.
My body won't cooperate!

I take it fore. I take it aft.
I want for more. I haven't laughed.
I'm such a bore. Can't find a date.
My body won't cooperate!

I take it near. I take it far.
I stop for beer at Harry's bar.
It's 3:00 a.m. No sleep's my fate.
My body won't cooperate!

I take it high. I take it low.
I heave a sigh. I've lost my glow.
I'm spinning down at such a rate.
My body won't cooperate!

I take it round. I take it straight.
I hear a tapping at my gate.
Should I get up or should I wait?
My body won't cooperate!

I take it fast. I take it slow.
I am aghast at how I grow.
I've reached a weight I really hate.
My body won't cooperate!

I take it far. I take it wide.
Hop in my car. Go for a ride.
I dread to walk at any gait.
My body won't cooperate!

I just don't know what's wrong with it—
My body's threatening to quit!!!
This albatross has been my fate.
My body won't cooperate!

✉ ✉ ✉

More Time with His Mercedes

I met a therapist one day
Who sat and shared with me,
"I counsel people of great wealth.
Their hardships do I see.

"The person that impressed me most
Had nothing left to gain.
Upon his deathbed he did lie
In misery and pain.

"My goal it was to comfort him
As he approached his end.
He'd been a faithful client of mine
And had become a friend.

"He said to me with great regret,
'I wish I hadn't spent
My precious time on worldly things
That cost a pretty cent.

'It's not the money or the fame
(Two things I've grown to hate)
That constitute what life's about
And now it's just too late.

'I cannot reconstruct the past.
Oh, how I wish I could!
I need my relatives and friends.
They'd do me so much good.

3

'I'd make them my priority.
I'd tell them how I felt.
I'd let myself be vulnerable,
Allow my heart to melt.

'Mercedes, stocks and large estate
Mean nothing to me now.
They can't bestow the love I need.
To riches I have bowed.

'Relationships are paramount.
"Important things" are not.
Please live your life for those you love.
True love cannot be bought.'

"And as I sat as therapist
And eased his lonely heart,
Without a friend or relative,
This man would soon depart.

"I never will forget that day.
So much from him I learned—
To live today the type of life
For which I've always yearned."

This story told, the therapist
And I in silence sat.
No words between us could be said
More meaningful than that.

✒ ✒ ✒

4

Closet Cleaning Phobia

Do you have that nasty closet
That just stares at you and says,
"Bet you never will come near me
'Cause I'm such an ugly mess"?

Lurking deep in its dominion,
Who could fathom what's beneath?
Maybe old stuff. Maybe new stuff.
Worn out sweatshirt, plastic wreath…

An aversion do we harbor
To clean out this closet full.
It's as if we have a phobia
And away from it we pull.

But today's the day I've promised
I will open up that door
And attempt to clean that closet
From the ceiling to the floor.

Okay, now I will get started.
If I'm lucky, phone will ring
And I'll have a few more moments
To avoid this gruesome thing.

Well, the phone is not complying,
But a thirst is coming on.
I should go and get some water.
I'll be back before too long.

Looking through my kitchen window,
Sun is calling me to play.
Maybe I should save the closet
For a gloomy, rainy day.

So the closet with its mysteries,
Ever safe from human purge,
Lingers high on my "To Do" list,
If I ever get the urge.

✉ ✉ ✉

Life in the Fast Lane

Life in the fast lane—you have to be faster.
If you slow down, it will be a disaster.
Life in the fast lane—you have to be speeding.
If you slow down, someone else might be leading.
Life in the fast lane—you have to be higher.
If you slow down, they might make you retire.
Life in the fast lane—you have to be spinning.
But, in this whirlwind, are you really winning?

Cellphonitis

Cellphonitis is a plague,
A modern-day dilemma.
It can strike at any age
To Jim, or Jane or Jenna.

Are there symptoms? Yes there are,
Like water from a faucet.
I'll just tell you ten of them
So you'll know if you've got it.

Symptom one is that your cell
Phone's "on" and always open.
Every second of the day,
It's for a call you're hoping.

Symptom two is that your phone's
Affixed upon your earlobe.
Will it sound or is there text
Or is it on the ring mode?

Symptom three is that your life
Is public now before us
Dramatized by endless chats
That irritate or bore us.

Symptom four is that your phone
Voice seems to be much louder.
In the aisles we hear you from
The jello to the chowder.

Symptom five is that you crave
A mountain of attention.
Drop a big name now and then,
Important people mention.

Symptom six is that you fail
To think of other people.
At a wedding in a church
The phone rings up the steeple.

Symptom seven, watch out folks!
You're driving in your auto
Running stop lights, blocking lanes.
"Self-Centered" is your motto.

Symptom eight is that your bills
Are well beyond your limit,
But you still fall prey to ads
And every cell phone gimmick.

Symptom nine is that your mind
Cannot be found relaxing.
With a ring at any hour,
Your cell phone can be taxing.

Symptom ten is that you think
That "free time" is just "dead space."
Free time is so scary, you
Replace it with the rat race.

There you have ten symptoms of
The cellphonitis system.
Careful, now, or you could be
Its next ill-fated victim.

📠 📠 📠

Parceled Out for Everyone Else

Does it seem your life is parceled out
For everyone else?
That there's not a second left to have
Some time for yourself?

Chances are this grand dilemma's no
Illusion at all.
Could it be your situation's just
A big wake-up call?

If you feel your life is parceled out
With no space for you,
Take a moment. Reassess your life—
Think what you can do.

Be creative, be assertive. You
Can help make it right.
Waiting for a friend to save you might
Result in a fight.

We are given life itself and we—
And nobody else—
Have the power to make it right. So, friend,
Take care of yourself.

✉ ✉ ✉

A Day at the Races

Hurry now: Alarm has rung.
Faster now: The toast has sprung.
Worry now: The kids aren't done.
Move it now: Just hold your tongue.

Hurry now: The meeting's on.
Faster now: It takes too long.
Worry now: Control that yawn.
Move it now: You're just a pawn.

Hurry now: A luncheon date.
Faster now: You have to wait.
Worry now: The boss is late.
Move it now: What is your fate?

Hurry now: Report is due.
Faster now: Some golf with Lou.
Worry now: You're still not through.
Move it now: Your list just grew.

Hurry now: The kids need rides.
Faster now: Your teen confides.
Worry now: The coach derides.
Move it now: You're taking sides.

Hurry now: The kids are fed.
Faster now: The homework's read.
Worry now: Where is your head?
Move it now: It's time for bed.
≢ ≢ ≢

Take a Break

Do you feel your brain is frying?
That a part of you is dying?
That your real self you're denying?
That you wish you were yourself?

Do you feel that you are drowning?
That your countenance is frowning?
That there's never time for clowning?
That you wish you were yourself?

When you get this awful feeling,
You can bet it's time for healing.
Give yourself a break from reeling
And you'll find you are yourself.

📧 📧 📧

Give Me A Pill

Purple pill, yellow pill, orange or red,
Give me a pill now or I'll lose my head.
I've just had chicken fried steak and a shake—
Feel like my stomach's an acid-filled lake!

Coated pill, extra-strength, large one or small,
Give me a pill now or I'll start to bawl.
I've just completed two marathon jogs—
Knees are collapsing and legs are like logs.

Over-the-counter or doctor prescribed,
Give me a pill now so I'll feel alive.
Can't get along without pills by my side.
Some I will show you and some I will hide.

Not long ago, pills did not so abound.
We'd take them just 'til we got off the ground.
Now we're accustomed to pharmacy lines.
Looks like pill-popping's a sign of our times.

✈ ✈ ✈

Remember the Kid

Remember the kid you brought into this world,
The one that you truly adore?
The one, when you enter your house after work,
Runs up with a hug at the door.

The one you consider the pride of your life.
The one with your eyes and your hair.
The one that you swore you would never neglect
But now find there's no time to care.

Well, that kid is changing, as sure as time flies.
With each passing day there is growth.
The time and attention you give to your child
Will nourish and comfort you both.

✉ ✉ ✉

Just Try Some Kindness

It's so easy to be burdened
With the problems of our days
That at times we are forgetful
Of the role that kindness plays.

Kindness—what a simple gesture,
Part of what we have to give.
But so often it gets buried
When we're not cooperative.

Funny thing about this kindness,
Once imparted, it will seem
That you actually feel better
And your countenance will beam.

Want a treat? Just try some kindness
On a stranger or a friend.
You will find your new self asking,
"When can I be kind again?"

✉ ✉ ✉

Fantasy Island

I woke up on Fantasy Island,
A marvelous sort of a place
Where beaches stretch miles in the distance
And blue skies drift off into space.

The warmth of the sun is disarming.
The sound of the waves brings a peace.
The air is abounding in pureness
And clouds are like soft tufts of fleece.

There are no computers or cell phones,
No faxes or telephone lines.
There is no congestion or rushing
And all that I wish for is mine.

I'll stay for a month on this island.
It's wonderful as it can be.
Please hold all my mail and appointments.
Returning, you'll find a new me.

✉ ✉ ✉

Whining and Dining

"Let's get together for dinner tonight."
"Okay, I'll meet you at eight."
"How 'bout Luigi's? That's good for a bite."
"So much to tell you. Can't wait!"

Dinner's fantastic and stories are told—
Chapters like acts from a play.
"Your boss did what! That's exceedingly bold.
What did you manage to say?"

Coffee drinks follow and details unfold
Really exposing the dirt.
Whining and dining are good for the soul,
'Specially over dessert.

✒ ✒ ✒

The Holiday Vow

Awhile ago did I endure a heinous holiday.
"How could it be so bad, my friend?" I now can hear
you say.
Well, I will tell you true, my friend, how much that
era hurt
In hopes that my experience you'll carefully avert.

It happened during Christmastime. So many things
to do.
Three months ahead did I begin preparing old and
new.
But then, I noticed things were piling up beyond
control
And reached a point where even all the good things
took a toll.

Some shopping here, some parties there, a potluck
dinner dish,
Some charities, some caroling, a child who made a
wish,
Some work, some home, some neighborhood, some
relatives and friends—
So packed with action was my life, it seemed to have
no end.

And one day in my living room, I stood and realized
That I was dying, melting down, right there before
    my eyes.
That moment, I did make a vow I've honored to this
    day:
To never let "too much to do" destroy a holiday.

✉ ✉ ✉

The Stressing Match

"You want to have a 'Stressing Match'?
Bet I'm more stressed than you.
I have a mortgage and three kids
And taxes now are due."

"Oh yeah? Well I've just leased a car.
My payments are a lot.
I also have a time-share due
That I regret I bought."

"Oh yeah? Well, there's a diamond ring
I just gave to my wife.
The money that I pay each month
Is ruining my life."

"Oh yeah, well I work 80 hours.
I rarely see the sun.
I feel I'm on a mission where
The battle's never won."

"Oh yeah, well try to raise three kids.
They really are a test!
At least before the day is done,
You have some time to rest."

"Okay, that's it. Let's call a truce.
This 'Stressing Match' is sick.
How 'bout we focus more on how
Our stresses can be licked?"

21

"Agreed! Let's have a 'Stress-Free Match'
And change our point of view.
We'll ease our stress, improve our life,
And carve out something new."

And so they met a month from then
And each one had good news.
The "Stress-Free Match" was won by both
Since neither one did lose!

✉ ✉ ✉

The Crumb de la Crumb

The crumb de la crumb look up:

The crumb de la crumb
Have fallen on the floor.
They're swept in a pan
And taken out the door.

The crumb de la crumb
Look up with great desire
At crème de la crème
Whose status is much higher.

The crumb de la crumb
Are always feeling lost.
They long to be prized
Instead of being tossed.

How great life would be
If only they were crème!
Their troubles would cease
If they could be like them.

The crème de la crème look down:

The crème de la crème
Must never ever sour.
They're up on the shelf
And over crumbs do tower.

The crème de la crème
Look down with great appeal
At crumb de la crumb
Who're trampled under heel.

The crème de la crème
Wish they could be below,
So simple and plain
And not just used for show.

How great life would be
If only they were crumbs!
Their troubles would cease
If they could live like bums.

🖅 🖅 🖅

Stopping on the Way

I went to the market and stopped on the way
  To pick up some stamps for Jean.
I parked at the cleaners and stopped on the way
  To pick up a magazine.
I drove to the market and stopped on the way
  To pick up some handy tools.
I turned right at Olsen's and stopped on the way
  To pick up my polished jewels.

I rode to the deli and stopped on the way
  To pick up some books for Len.
I went to the fruit stand and stopped on the way
  To pick up a cornish hen.
I crossed o'er the river and stopped on the way
  To pick up the latest news.
I veered toward the parkway and stopped on the way
  To pick up my walking shoes.

I entered the forest and stopped on the way
  To pick up how tired I'd grown.
I sat on a bench and invited the squirrels
  To pick up some nuts I'd thrown.
I looked straight above me and noticed the leaves
  Embracing the filtered sun.
I felt a connection with everything there
  Acknowledging we were one.

I found myself singing a never-sung song
  That echoed throughout the trees,
And felt such a wholeness in all of my being—
  A silhouette on a breeze.
My face lost its tension, my body relaxed.
  I heralded a new day.
And I am still singing that never-sung song
  I picked up along the way.

✉ ✉ ✉

Slow Down

Slow down,
Put your feet on the ground.
Slow down,
'Til a calmness is found.
Slow down,
Hear the tiniest sound.
Slow down,
There's a stillness around.

Slow down,
Take a leisurely walk.
Slow down,
Watch the crow; glimpse the hawk.
Slow down,
Touch a leaf; hold a rock.
Slow down,
Life's not based on the clock.

Slow down,
Let your senses be one.
Slow down,
Catch the rays of the sun.
Slow down,
Feel the air in your lungs.
Slow down,
Gently smile, just for fun.

Slow down,
When it's time to unwind.
Slow down,
Hear your heart with your mind.
Slow down,
To your body be kind.
Slow down,
Inner peace you will find.

Slow down,
When it's time for repose.
Slow down,
Each day comes to a close.
Slow down,
Shed your joys and your woes.
Sleep now,
Slumber's soft as a rose.

📧 📧 📧

I Can't Wait!

I can't wait for slow things!

I can't wait in line.
The cab's not on time
The food takes too long.
The teller is wrong.
The copier's slow.
I'm stuck in this row.
There's never enough.
Life's always so tough.

I can't wait for good things!

The good stuff won't last.
Vacation's too fast.
I can't wait for spring.
Why won't the phone ring?
There's just so much food.
I'm not in the mood.
Can't wait for a break.
How much can I take?

I can't wait for bad things!

A storm's in the works.
The dentist date lurks.
It's risky outside.
I know I can't hide.

I'm destined to fail.
I'm drowning in mail.
Divorce will come soon.
Tonight's a full moon.

I can't wait for anything!

Why can't things just pass
Instead of harass?
Why can't life occur
In one cosmic blur?
It's never just right.
I'm always uptight.
Life's so hard to take.
Why? 'Cause I can't wait!!!

✉ ✉ ✉

I've Lost My Calendar

I've lost my calendar. I've lost my mind.
It seems the universe is so unkind.
I barely function now with datebook gone.
I'd recreate it all, but I'd be wrong.

I've lost my calendar. I've lost my mind.
Tomorrow panics me because I'm blind.
I'm like a ship at sea without a sail,
Or like a train that's destined to derail.

I've lost my calendar. I've lost my mind.
It's hard to reconstruct what I can't find.
I have no memory of what's ahead.
I can't remember what I wrote or said.

I've found my calendar! I've found my mind!
It seems the universe is oh so kind.
I've aged a decade, but at least I'm sane.
I swear that datebook won't be lost again!

The Convention of Conventions

Next year, the Convention of Conventions
Will be held in our neighborhood.
All this, so we'll know what's right and wrong and
Be correct, as we always should.

First off, should the toilet paper ends be
Facing in or be facing out?
Second, should the color of the socks match
Pants or shoes? We'll erase all doubt.

Thirdly, should we eat three meals a day or
Many more? What do doctors say?
Fourthly, is the tie clip or the stickpin
Best to wear? We'll decide that day.

All this and so many crucial topics
Will be touched in a one-day span.
Right here, the Convention of Conventions
In our midst! Be there if you can!

✉ ✉ ✉

The Crazy List Loop

There's a list on the fridge.
There's a list in the car.
There's a list on the table
And one in the bar.

There's a list on the bed.
There's a list in the drawer.
There's a list on the mirror
And one on the floor.

There's a list on my desk.
There's a list in my coat.
There's a list on my dresser
And one in my boat.

There's a list in my book.
There's a list on my sink.
There's a list in my pocket
And one by my drink.

There's a list on my chair.
There's a list in my den.
There's a list in my folder.
Where was it again?

Was the list on my bed?
Was the list in my soup?
Now, I'm getting confused
In the crazy list loop!

No Turn on Red

I looked at the sign above me,
"No Turn on Red."
I wondered how long I'd be there.
"Patience," I said.

I noticed some pigeons pecking,
Searching the ground.
Five pigeons in need of food but
No seeds were found.

I glared at the sign and glowered,
"I will be late."
I knew if I ran the stop sign,
Ticket was fate.

No wonder the birds were hunting
With eager beaks.
The season would soon be ending.
Food source was bleak.

I then saw some people gather.
Pigeons did flee.
It turned out this was a bus stop
Under a tree.

I glanced in the rearview mirror—
No cars behind.
How this could be true at rush hour
Strange I did find.

Then flew in one lonely pigeon,
Brave of the flock,
That was not intimidated
By human stock.

The time on the dashboard clock read
Ten after five.
The thought of illegal turning
Now came alive.

A girl then approached the stop and
Entered the fold.
From under a hat her hair flowed
Auburn and gold.

She drew from a paper bag a
Small piece of bread
And tore off such tiny morsels—
Birds would be fed.

The lone bird was still in sight and
Near her it flew.
By instinct it knew to trust her.
Confidence grew.

Each breadcrumb it ate, then sweetly
Tilted its head
To look at its kind provider,
"Thank you," it said.

The bus people stared and watched as
This did unfold,
A non-story story plot that
Now could be told.

I finally made the turn and
Forged on ahead,
But carried that sign within me,
"No Turn on Red."

≢ ≢ ≢

When, Then

When I select the best exercise plan,
Then will my body do all that it can.
When I can choose the right diet for me,
Then will I lose weight, you just wait and see.

When I can find time to play with my boy,
Then will he know me beyond the bought toy.
When I can spend time with husband or wife,
Then we'll rekindle the love of our life.

When I can take an adventurous trip,
Then from the cup of excitement I'll sip.
When I have saved up enough to be set,
Then will I find out what money can get.

When I can manage to get off my seat,
Then will I buy decent shoes for my feet.
When I have legroom, enough to spread out,
Then will I clean up and turn things about.

When I retire, before I grow old,
Then will my leisure time start to unfold.
When I'm a senior, I'll work on some art,
Then I'll be able to nurture my heart.

When I can know all that I need to know,
Then will I venture out fearless of foe.
When I am certain I won't shed a tear,
Then will I live my life empty of fear.

When I can get truth from those who have lied,
Then will I give myself what's been denied.
When I meet just the right person for me,
Then will my days be unfettered and free.

'Til then, I'll just have to muddle along
Hoping my weariness won't end my song.

✉ ✉ ✉

Are You Somebody Else?

Are you really you, or just somebody else?
Are you really true, or is "you" on the shelf?
When you look at you, is it you that you see?
If you look real close, do you find you or me?

When you have to choose, do you dare to decide?
Do you do what's right, or just shrink back and hide?
Do you use your talents and bloom in your place?
Or linger behind and then feel you're erased?

Do you dream your dream, or do you drift away?
Do you hear your words, or just what others say?
Do you live the full life that you're meant to live?
Do you trust enough to give all you can give?

🖃 🖃 🖃

More Than You Can Chew

You've taken on more than you can chew.
Oh, this is great!
You've learned to take risks with something new.
Never too late!

You've taken on more than you can chew.
Oh, this is hard!
Dilemmas and chaos do ensue.
Gut feels like lard!

You've taken on more than you can chew.
Oh, this is bad!
You're totally stressed—too much to do.
You're always mad!

You've taken on more than you can chew.
Oh, this is great!
You've learned to let go of what can wait.
Never too late!

📧 📧 📧